John W. Schaum
Note Story Spelling Book

Preface

This unique writing book consists of a series of attractive stories in which many of the words appear in music notation so that the student will need to read notes in order to understand the story. Much of the subject matter is based on fact or interesting American legends.

The *Note Story Spelling Book* is suitable for elementary-level students in their first or second year of study. This music speller may be used for instrumental students, piano students, or general classroom use. The contents provide the means of drilling students on note reading in both a fun and motivating way.

The stories may be used in three ways:

1. As a reader: The student may simply read the stories.
2. As a note speller: The student writes out the letter names.
3. As a performance book: The student plays the notes on the piano.

Editor: Gail Lew
Production Coordinator: Sheryl Rose
Art Layout: Martha Ramirez
Cover Illustration: Magdi Rodríguez
Interior Illustrations: Magdi Rodríguez and Joseph R. Redka

John W. Schaum
Note Story Spelling Book

CONTENTS

Space Ship

Hans Christian Andersen

Hans was born in the vill- [♪] of Odense in [♪] -nmark.

His [♪] -mily was too poor to [♪] -ucate him properly. His [♪]

was a shoemaker and his mother wash- [♪] clothes. Hans loved the st- [♪] and

m- [♪] many [♪] -orts to [♪] -t into th- [♪] -ter work.

However he n- [♪] an [♪] -ucation [♪] -ly. Finally some

of his friends agr- [♪] to help him. They m- [♪] it possible for him to go

to an [♪] -my to [♪] -t some knowl- [♪] . At 14, he

[♪] -i- [♪] to go to Copenh- [♪] n. [♪] -ter three

y- [♪] -rs of [♪] fortune, he finally [♪] -me to the attention of a

th- [♪] -ter director who h- [♪] [♪] -ith in Hans' [♪] -ility.

This [♪] -n to chan- [♪] his luck. He is most [♪] -mous

for his [♪] -iry tales such as the R- [♪] Shoes and the Ugly Duckling.

EL00579A

Football Finger Man

-orge is a -mous football who -n throw long passes that win -ll -mes. Piano playing m- his fingers strong and -le to spr- firmly around the -ll. If the other t- -m is in the l- , the quarter- -k -lls signals telling -orge to -t r- -y to pass. Our hero pl- -s a -uty. The right end player -tches it and r- -s for a much n- touchdown. The -s of the crowd are -ming with -light. This turned the ti- and soon he goes ah- with another well pl- pass that saves the t- -m from -t. This is a true story showing how a knowl- of piano help- a football

Paleface Becomes Indian

A white man nam- [music] Laubin [music] -i- [music]

to [music] -ome a member of the Sioux Indian tri- [music]

He h- [music] a [music] -p [music] -tion for Indian [music] -nces and

m- [music] a [music] -reer of performing these [music] -nces on the

st- [music] throughout the land. The Chi- [music] [music] -stowed a high

honor on Laubin when he [music] -ve him the name "One Bull." He [music] -lled

him "One Bull" [music] -use he was alone in this work. Laubin m- [music]

himself look like the r- [music] skins by dressing in their [music] -thered

costumes. He liv- [music] in an Indian vill- [music] and [music] -ined a lot

of knowl- [music] [music] -out Indian li- [music]

Truly, here is a pale- [music] who [music] -me an Indian.

Paul Bunyan

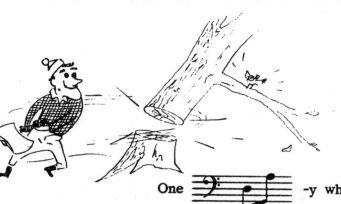

One [♪] -y when Paul was working in his [♪] 's

logging [♪] -mp it [♪] -n to snow. It snowed st- [♪] -ily

for [♪] -ys. Finally the whole pl- [♪] [♪] -me covered.

Log [♪] -ins and tr- [♪] -s were buri- [♪] in the

[♪] -p drifts. [♪] -ter the storm, Paul pro- [♪]

to look for firewood. He noti- [♪] two [♪] -rs sticking up

through a snowdrift. He r- [♪] -hed down with his hu- [♪]

hands and pull- [♪] the thing out of the snow. It was a [♪] -y

ox [♪] -lf with thin wo- [♪] -ly l- [♪] 's. Paul put the [♪] -lf

in one of his pockets and h- [♪] home. He [♪] the [♪] -y;

ox warm milk in front of the firepl- [♪] He nam- [♪] the

[♪] -lf [♪] and [♪] -i- [♪] to keep him for a pet.

Mid-Ocean Mercy Mission

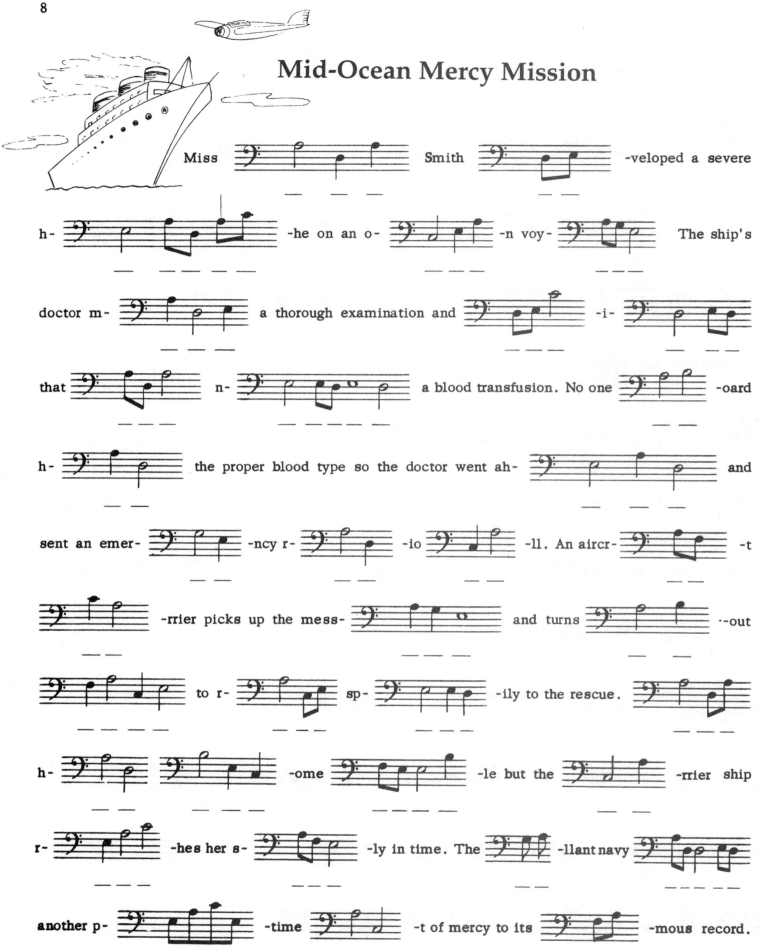

The White House Squirrels

One [♪] -y a young l- [♪] nam- [♪] [♪] -nny

was p- [♪] -ing by the White House lawn. He noti- [♪] the [♪] -t

that the squirrels s- [♪] -med thin and h- [♪] a hungry look

[♪] -out them. The i- [♪] entered his h- [♪] to go in and

con- [♪] -r with the President. "The squirrels n- [♪] more to [♪] -t.

They aren't [♪] -t enough," said [♪] -nny. The President

agr- [♪] that something h- [♪] to [♪] done but without

[♪] -using a tax incr- [♪] -se. So he m- [♪] [♪] -nny the official

[♪] -r but said "The government [♪] -n't [♪] -ord to pay

you [♪] ." But so [♪] -p was [♪] -nny's [♪] -tion

for the squirrels that he gl- [♪] -ly [♪] -pted. He sp- [♪] -ily got a

[♪] of nuts r- [♪] -y, and went out to [♪] -in [♪] -ing his pets.

The Wrestling Match

EL00579A

11,000 Mile Bike Hike

NOTE: Be careful! Treble and bass clefs are intermingled.

Bear Facts

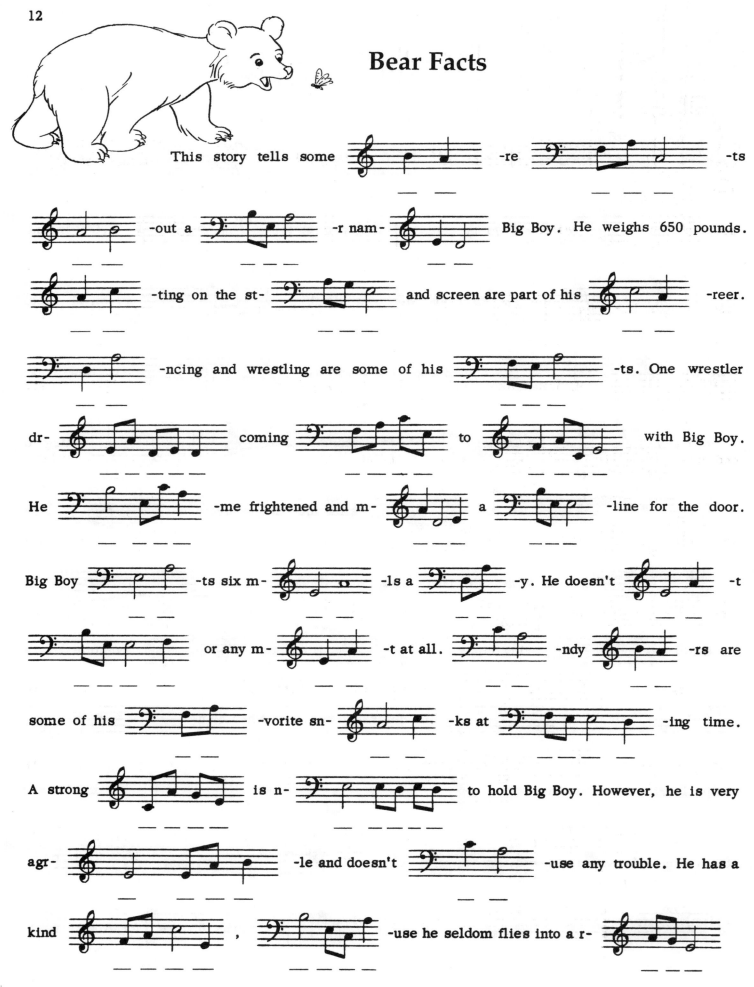

This story tells some ♪ -re 𝄢 ♪ -ts

-out a 𝄢 ♪ -r nam- ♪ Big Boy. He weighs 650 pounds.

-ting on the st- 𝄢 ♪ and screen are part of his ♪ -reer.

𝄢 -ncing and wrestling are some of his 𝄢 ♪ -ts. One wrestler

dr- ♪ coming 𝄢 ♪ to ♪ with Big Boy.

He 𝄢 ♪ -me frightened and m- ♪ a 𝄢 ♪ -line for the door.

Big Boy 𝄢 -ts six m- ♪ -ls a 𝄢 ♪ -y. He doesn't ♪ -t

𝄢 ♪ or any m- ♪ -t at all. 𝄢 -ndy ♪ -rs are

some of his 𝄢 ♪ -vorite sn- ♪ -ks at 𝄢 ♪ -ing time.

A strong ♪ is n- 𝄢 ♪ to hold Big Boy. However, he is very

agr- ♪ -le and doesn't 𝄢 ♪ -use any trouble. He has a

kind ♪ , 𝄢 ♪ -use he seldom flies into a r- ♪

The Submerged Cavern

-ter diving more than 150

un- -r water, a young coll- stu- -nt

discovered a hu- -vern in a -p

-lifornia lake. He -rried a -mera

and us- strong flashlight while s- -rching

the -pths. He h- on a ru- -r suit and

us- sp- -ial br- thing tu- -s.

A strong slen- -r cord was ti- to his waist

and this was n- to pull him up s- -ly

to the sur- . This was a gr- -t

and a lot to scientific knowl-

Zozobra

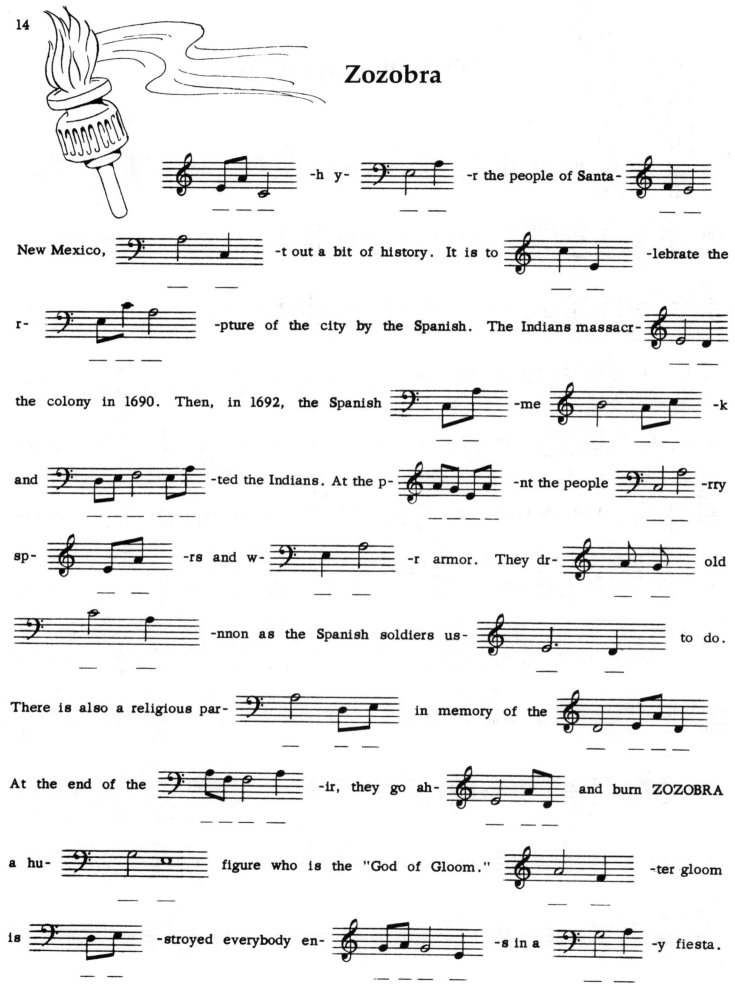

(music notation) -h y- (music notation) -r the people of Santa- (music notation)

New Mexico, (music notation) -t out a bit of history. It is to (music notation) -lebrate the

r- (music notation) -pture of the city by the Spanish. The Indians massacr- (music notation)

the colony in 1690. Then, in 1692, the Spanish (music notation) -me (music notation) -k

and (music notation) -ted the Indians. At the p- (music notation) -nt the people (music notation) -rry

sp- (music notation) -rs and w- (music notation) -r armor. They dr- (music notation) old

(music notation) -nnon as the Spanish soldiers us- (music notation) to do.

There is also a religious par- (music notation) in memory of the (music notation)

At the end of the (music notation) -ir, they go ah- (music notation) and burn ZOZOBRA

a hu- (music notation) figure who is the "God of Gloom." (music notation) -ter gloom

is (music notation) -stroyed everybody en- (music notation) -s in a (music notation) -y fiesta.

The Kentucky Derby

The K-9 Corps

Homemade Submarine

R- [♪] -ntly two [♪] -ntists (brothers)

complet- [♪] a submarine which they m- [♪] in their

[♪] -sement. They h- [♪] [♪] -n building it for

thr- [♪] y- [♪] -rs. The r- [♪] -l test [♪] -me

when they truck- [♪] it down to a water-filled quarry in Al- [♪] -ma.

The whole town of Birmingham was [♪] -r to s- [♪] if it

would work. Slowly it pro- [♪] to [♪] launched

down sp- [♪] -ial tr- [♪] -ks into the [♪] -p

waters. The brothers hopp- [♪] in and m- [♪] local history

when it su- [♪] in coming up s- [♪] -ly.

It h- [♪] a [♪] -le attachment so that a sur- [♪]

cr- [♪] -t could dr- [♪] it out in an emer- [♪] -ncy.

The World's Largest Bell

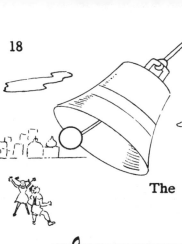

The bi- -st -ll on -rth is to found in Moscow. It is -ll- the "emperor of bells". This hu- bell weighs -out 219 tons and its si- -s are thr- -t thick. It m- -sures almost 23 -t -ross at its -se and r- -hes a height of over 19 feet. Very little knowl- -n found out -out it. It pro- -ly crash- -ter -ing hung -use it lay in a hole for more than a -ntury. In 1836, it was rais- and m- into a chapel. The dam- s- -tion of the -ll has -n m- into a doorway.

Buried Treasure

Buffalo Bill

Bill was a l- [note] eleven y- [note] -rs of [note] , his [note] h- [note] just di- [note] and his [note] -mily n- [note] money so he was for- [note] to [note] -t out and [note] -rn a living. He su- [note] in [note] -tting a job with a cover- [note] w- [note] -on train h- [note] --ing west. He told his boss that he could ri- [note] short and herd [note] -ttle. On the way the w- [note] -on train was att- [note] -ked by a lar- [note] tri- [note] of Indians. The only m- [note] -ns of es- [note] -pe was to follow the str- [note] -m. As they tru- [note] on, Bill l- [note] [note] -hind. Su- [note] -nly he saw an Indian r- [note] -y to shoot an arrow. Bill aim- [note] -refully, and killed him with one shot. This [note] -ve the men. ah- [note] a warning so they were [note] -le to hold off the att- [note] -k.

Fun in a Helicopter

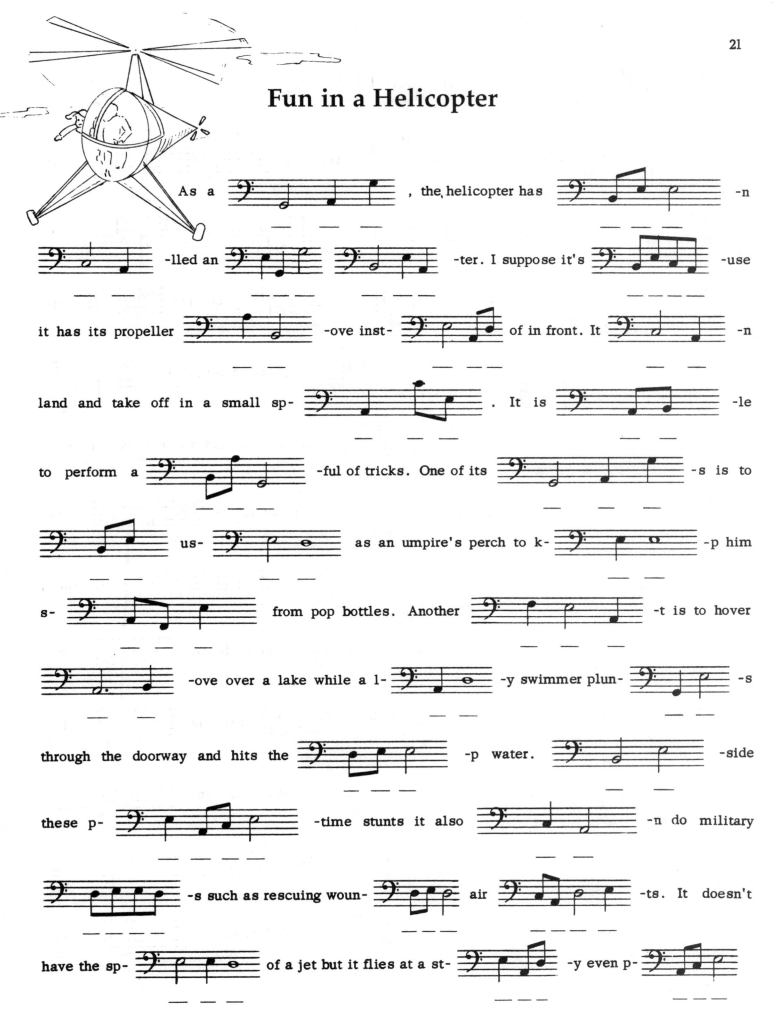

An Animal That Swims Backward

Three-Ring Circus

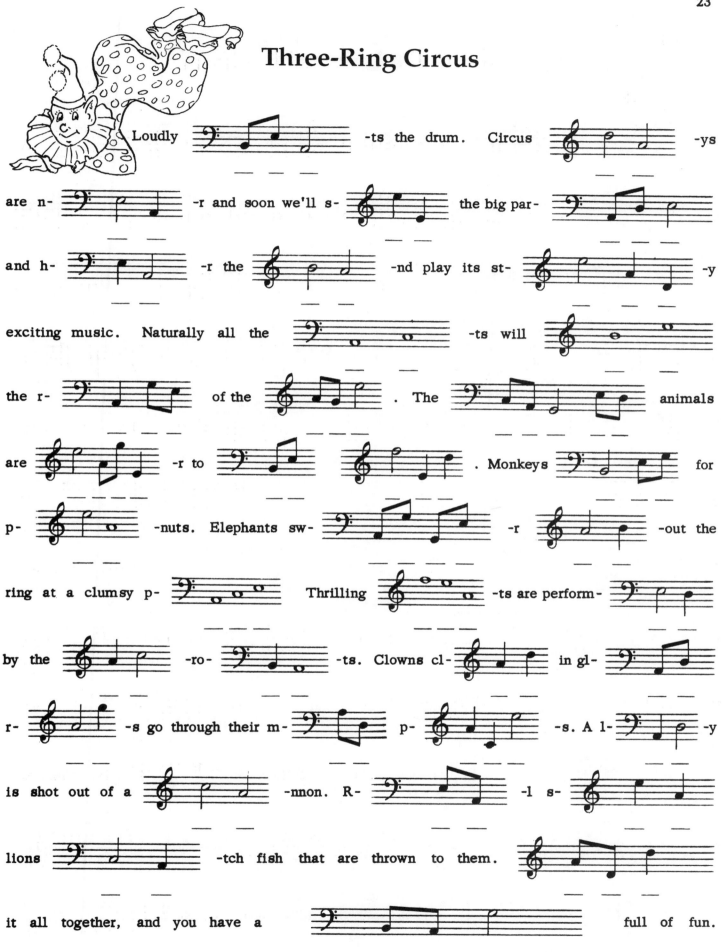

Loudly ⟨notes⟩ -ts the drum. Circus ⟨notes⟩ -ys are n- ⟨notes⟩ -r and soon we'll s- ⟨notes⟩ the big par- ⟨notes⟩ and h- ⟨notes⟩ -r the ⟨notes⟩ -nd play its st- ⟨notes⟩ -y exciting music. Naturally all the ⟨notes⟩ -ts will ⟨notes⟩ the r- ⟨notes⟩ of the ⟨notes⟩ . The ⟨notes⟩ animals are ⟨notes⟩ -r to ⟨notes⟩ ⟨notes⟩ . Monkeys ⟨notes⟩ for p- ⟨notes⟩ -nuts. Elephants sw- ⟨notes⟩ -r ⟨notes⟩ -out the ring at a clumsy p- ⟨notes⟩ Thrilling ⟨notes⟩ -ts are perform- ⟨notes⟩ by the ⟨notes⟩ -ro- ⟨notes⟩ -ts. Clowns cl- ⟨notes⟩ in gl- ⟨notes⟩ r- ⟨notes⟩ -s go through their m- ⟨notes⟩ p- ⟨notes⟩ -s. A l- ⟨notes⟩ -y is shot out of a ⟨notes⟩ -nnon. R- ⟨notes⟩ -l s- ⟨notes⟩ lions ⟨notes⟩ -tch fish that are thrown to them. ⟨notes⟩ it all together, and you have a ⟨notes⟩ full of fun.

EL00579A

Turkey vs. Eagle

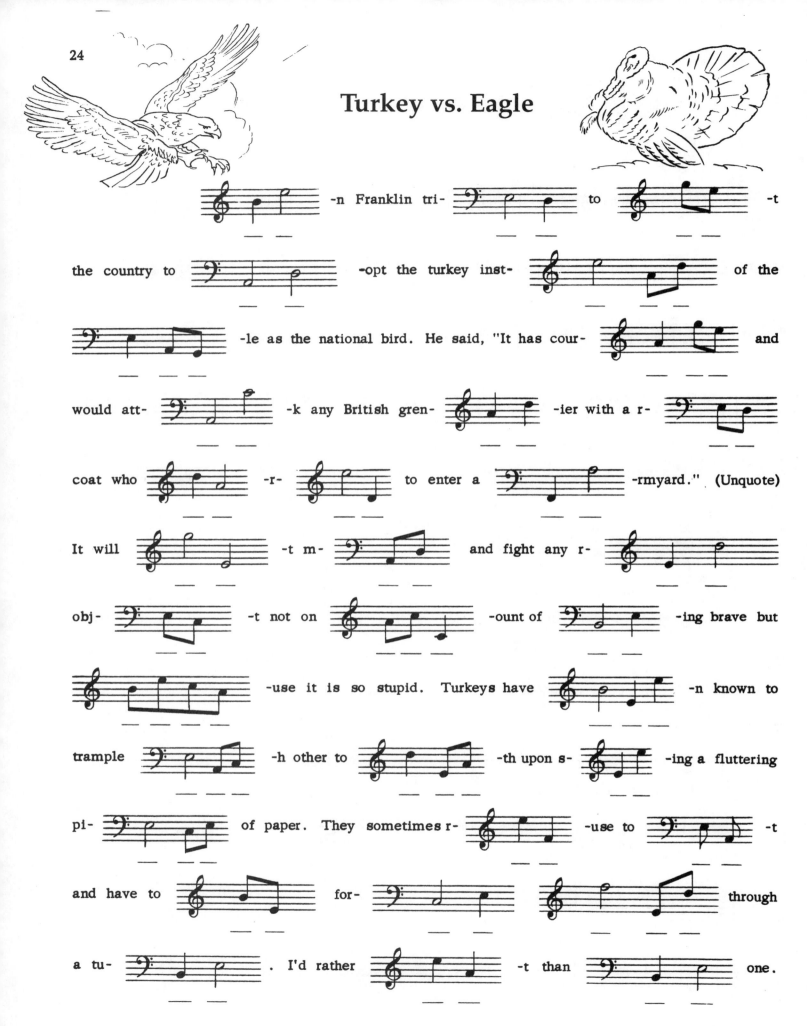

[♪] -n Franklin tri- [♪] to [♪] -t the country to [♪] -opt the turkey inst- [♪] of the [♪] -le as the national bird. He said, "It has cour- [♪] and would att- [♪] -k any British gren- [♪] -ier with a r- [♪] coat who [♪] -r- [♪] to enter a [♪] -rmyard." (Unquote) It will [♪] -t m- [♪] and fight any r- [♪] obj- [♪] -t not on [♪] -ount of [♪] -ing brave but [♪] -use it is so stupid. Turkeys have [♪] -n known to trample [♪] -h other to [♪] -th upon s- [♪] -ing a fluttering pi- [♪] of paper. They sometimes r- [♪] -use to [♪] -t and have to [♪] for- [♪] [♪] through a tu- [♪] . I'd rather [♪] -t than [♪] one.

Tragedy on the Plains

Mardi Gras

Radar Patrol

It is now l- [♪] -l in s- [♪] -tions of the country to use r- [♪] -r as a m- [♪] -ns of [♪] -tting evi- [♪] -nce [♪] -inst sp- [♪] -ing. The [♪] -st driver must [♪] -ware. A tr- [♪] -ic cop [♪] -n arrest a [♪] -r driver on the [♪] -sis of information obtain- [♪] by r- [♪] -io from another o- [♪] -icer who has s- [♪] -n by m- [♪] -ns of r- [♪] -r the sp- [♪] of the motorist to [♪] arrest- [♪] This is a good i- [♪] and should help to make [♪] -idents [♪] away. Radar is a mo- [♪] -l of how a military [♪] -vi- [♪] [♪] -n [♪] used for a p- [♪] -time [♪] -use. Inst- [♪] of r- [♪] -ing -ter sp- [♪] -rs, radar now [♪] -nds the public s- [♪] -ty.

Ships That Crash in the Night

Davy Crockett

Lincoln's Totem Pole

Quiz

DIRECTIONS: On the staffs below, you are to write a whole note above

each of the underlined letters. Use as many different locations as possible.

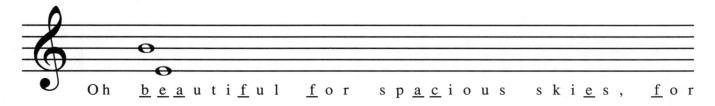

Oh b̲eauti̲ful f̲or spac̲ious ski̲es, f̲or

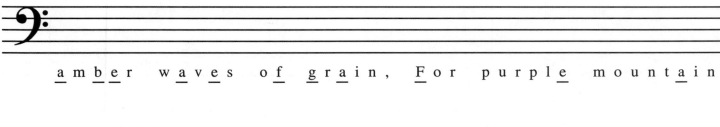

a̲mb̲er wa̲ve̲s o̲f g̲ra̲in, For purpl̲e mounta̲in

ma̲je̲sti̲es A̲b̲ove̲ the̲ f̲ruite̲d pla̲in.

A̲m̲e̲rica̲! A̲m̲e̲rica̲! G̲o̲d̲ she̲d̲ his g̲ra̲ce̲

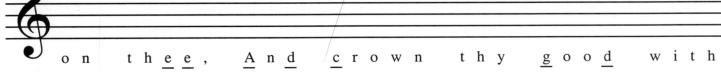

on the̲e̲, A̲n̲d̲ c̲rown thy g̲o̲o̲d̲ with

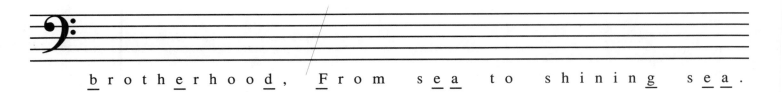

b̲rothe̲rhood̲, F̲rom se̲a̲ to shining se̲a̲.

John W. Schaum
(1905–1988)

Founder and director of the Schaum Music School in Milwaukee, Wisconsin, John W. Schaum is the composer of internationally famous piano teaching materials including more than 200 books and 450 sheet music pieces. He is author of the internationally acclaimed *Schaum Piano Course* published by Belwin-Mills Publishing Corporation/Warner Bros. Publications. During his extensive travels, Mr. Schaum presented hundreds of piano teacher workshops in all fifty states. He was president of the Wisconsin Music Teachers Association and soloist with the Milwaukee Philharmonic Orchestra.

Mr. Schaum received a master of music degree from Northwestern University, a bachelor of music degree from Marquette University, and a bachelor of music education degree from the University of Wisconsin-Milwaukee.

He remains an important influence in the lives of hundreds of thousands of piano students who have enjoyed and continue to play his music.